Introduction to
Trees as a Theme

Trees have long held a fascination and at full awe inspiring height can dominate the landscape and overshadow all living things. It is not surprising that in many ancient cultures they were endowed with spiritual significance.

In Genesis, the Garden of Eden is described as the place where "the Lord God made all kinds of trees grow out of the ground – trees that were pleasing to the eye and good for food. In the middle of the garden were the tree of life and the tree of the knowledge of good and evil".

The ancient Egyptians also believed in the tree of life and tomb paintings depict the sap as rising up through the earth and the trunk and out through the crown of the tree as an elixir of life and the key to immortality.

Traditions concerning the tree of life abound throughout the world in a wide range of cultures and the diverse imagery is a wonderful source of pattern and design for artists.

Piet Mondrian made an intensive study of trees for five years and became fascinated with the structure of the tree form, gradually paring down the elements to verticals and horizontals which could perhaps be seen as the warp and weft of life.

Some trees have legends and superstitions associated with them. Wych elm is a healer and the yew can be unlucky as it is symbolic of death and the underworld. It is also unlucky to harm the oak as it represents strength and healing. 'Touching wood' or 'knocking on wood' are phrases in daily use and are superstitions from ancient times thought to refer to appeasing the powerful tree spirit.

The historical perspective is just one of the aspects of trees that could provide a lifetime of inspiration.

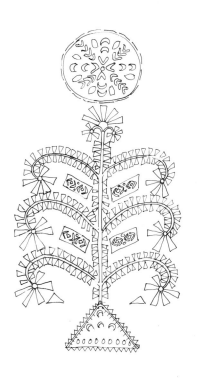

Inside front cover: *Large organic shapes growing all over the tree trunk displayed a variety of textures- bumpy, smooth, tufted and coloured apple, olive, emerald and acid yellow greens.*

Snippets of fabric and thread were bonded to a fabric painted ground cloth. Some puff paint was applied before the top chiffon was bonded in place which expanded when heat was applied. Hand and machine stitches linked and accentuated some of the textures. Coloured dimensional fabric paint was applied to incorporate the stitching to the background. (JB)

Right: *Sketches of an apple tree in late Autumn, a pollarded tree and a symbolic Tree of Life from the Greek Islands. (JB)*

Looking at Trees

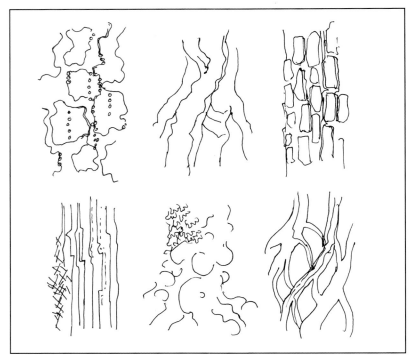

Quick diagrams showing the general characteristics of varying tree bark. (JB)

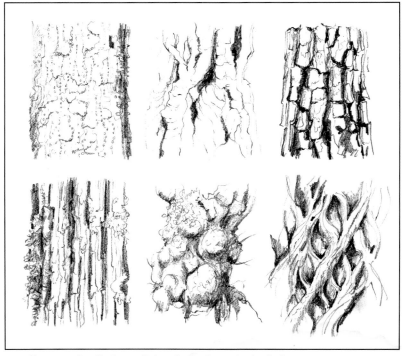

Pencil - more detailed pencil drawings of tree bark. (JB)

We all think that we really observe things but so often it can be superficial. It is said that 'it is easy to look but not so easy to see'. For instance, if anyone, regardless of age, is asked to describe or paint the colour of a tree trunk many would suggest grey or brown. A more focused look will reveal that the colours of many trees range from silvery white, apricot or rich crimson through to maroon.

The most helpful thing to do is to discipline your looking in order to improve your enjoyment of things around you, your observational skills, reference and ultimately your creativity. These experiences can go on to inspire descriptive writing, poetry, painting or stitched textiles.

To illustrate this point, initially select some trees on which to focus for several weeks. On your walk remember to take a small notebook and pencil with binoculars and a camera as optional extras.

In the first instance, as you approach a particular tree, describe the general colour of the bark. Is it grey, brown or beige? As you walk closer, can you add more details to your first impressions? Perhaps mid grey, silvery, charcoal, pearl or greeny grey may be more accurate colourings. If the tree trunk is brown, is it rusty coloured, greyish or gingery? Alternatively a beige tree may include peach, straw coloured tints or even a hint of a pinky tinge. Closer inspection may reveal delightful and unexpected additional colours within the bark, or mosses, lichen or fungi adhered to it.

Try and describe the colours accurately as you see them. The proportions of colour one to another are also important. Once armed with this information you can always choose to disregard certain elements and exaggerate or understate others as your designs develop. One description found in a notebook reads: 'At first glance the surface of the tree was a dull pearl grey but a closer inspection revealed a hint of dirty peach. There were rusty pink areas alongside dark and mid greys. Tiny flashes or dots of lime green contrasted with areas of frilly greyish turquoise lichen, which was beginning to envelop several branches.'

Having recorded some notes on colour schemes you can now concentrate on looking at the surface textures.

• Is the bark smooth, ridged, twisted, patchy, scaly, encrusted or creviced?

• Do any markings on the bark appear to meander over the surface, vertically patterned in deep creases or furrows or wrap around the trunk in horizontal bands like bandages or ribbons?

• Which other features appeal to you? Peeling scaly bark, insect ravaged structures, wart like growths or pollarded protrubencies may all be intriguing.

• Select a section of bark and make some quick diagrams with descriptive notes. Do not attempt a 'proper' drawing in the first instance; just jot a few lines to capture the main characteristics of the patterns or markings. Add notes describing the colour and surface textures. Undulating, broken, gashed, gnarled, ribboned, blasted, latticed, holey, spiralled, could all be helpful words to note.

• First impressions and jottings could be followed by more detailed observations. Aquarelle pencils (where clear water can be added to make a wash), a range of B pencils for intensified tones, or collaged papers could also be tried (see pages 4,5&16).

This procedure can progress to describing the overall shape of particular trees. Some like poplar trees are tall, slim, elegant with upward growing branches, whereas some oak trees are more stately, broad, with a spreading growth. By contrast branches of some willow trees drape and bow down. The list is endless.

As seasons pass, leaves, flowers, fruits and seeds can swell your bank of reference. Once armed with this knowledge, the choice of development is yours. The delicate green and pink colour scheme to be seen on the clusters of winged seeds from a field maple tree could inspire a machine embroidery whereas their shapes could be repeated into an overall pattern for a quilting project.

You will have enough information to depict literal or impressionistic images, or by exaggerating some aspects and understating others, stylised, semi abstract or abstract patterns can emerge.

Aquarelle crayon and pencil drawing showing a ridged tree bark with lichen. (JB)

Recording Information - Black & White

We know that drawing is the best way to reinforce thorough and structured looking. Photographs can assist but drawing offers the most useful information. Drawing can take many forms and with a robust subject such as textured tree bark simple mark making and printing in black and white can describe the patterns and textures with energy and strength.

There is a wide range of black and white media available and a little time spent making marks with a variety of pencils, particularly the soft B range will demonstrate an array of qualities and intensity. Fibre tip pens, ballpoint pens, wedged italic pens etc. could be useful either individually or in combination.

• Graphite is good for strong rhythmic shapes particularly 6B or softer. Select an area of tree bark and analyse the direction and quality of the patterns and use graphite strokes to indicate movement and texture. A putty rubber can then be used to work into the graphite marks for powerful effects. With this method it is possible to really extend the marks and emphasise the rhythms. (See far right)

Experiment with different types of paper and backgrounds. Soft paper will inhibit the putty rubber whereas a smooth or shiny surface will enable sweeping marks to be made. Wrapping paper, tissue paper, cartridge and watercolour paper each have special qualities for differing results.

• Drawing on crumpled paper will offer an exciting surface for drawing.

• With dry media an interesting fractured line may well enrich the image and with wet media the ink may seep into the cracks where the surface of the paper has been broken down and this can be most effective.

• Combination surfaces are most exciting and a rough collage of newspaper or magazine shapes can be painted over with white acrylic paint and allowed to dry before drawing. (left)

• Manipulated paper, particularly when using monochrome will encourage a good understanding of the dimensional surface of the bark and acts as a bridge between the literal and interpretive recording of information.
(see page 7)

• Twigs dripped in ink may well describe the structures of tree bark most effectively.

• Many people find mixtures of printed marks a sympathetic method of recording information. Foam sponge is excellent for soft textures. The edge of a piece of card is also useful not only for making linear marks but for dragging into interesting effects.

Working in black and white can encourage a focus on the structure and patterns of the subject and colour can be added to further enrich the studies.

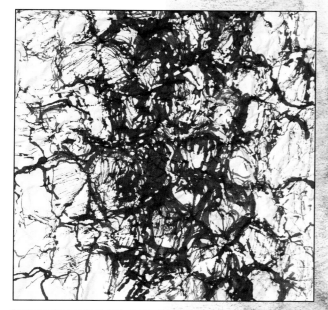

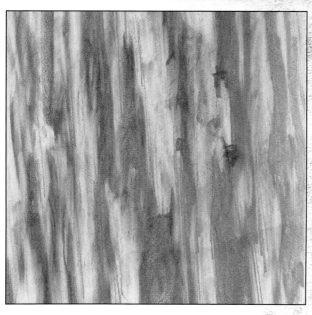

Far left: A freely applied newspaper collage over painted with acrylic paint formed the background for this graphite interpretation of tree bark. The plastic rubber marks worked into the graphite drawing reinforced the vigour of the surface.

Top left: Crumpled cartridge paper offers an interesting surface for textured drawing. A twig dipped in ink was used to draw the patterns which echo the textural marks of the tree bark.

Middle: This tree bark drawing was worked entirely by printing with the edge of a piece of card dipped in black acrylic paint.

Bottom left: Graphite on shiny paper allows smooth rhythmic marks of the plastic rubber into the drawing. (JL)

Developing a Theme - Mixed Media

Design developments based on the tree reference help to bridge the gap between careful observation and interpretation. Collage is a good starting point as it demands a simplification of shape. Any aspect of the source can be exaggerated at this point. The colour can be enhanced, the patterns simplified, and the elements composed into various designs.

The collage papers could include colour magazines, self coloured tissue papers, the papers left from transfer painting (see Transfer to Transform) etc. Tearing works particularly well for organic forms. A mixture of paper and fabric is an effective way of simplifying and promoting interesting ideas. The palm tree texture (left) was constructed on a black plastic bin liner as support.

• The glue is loosely based on 1 part PVA glue to 10 parts water and a splattering of cellulose paste. It is possible to have more or less glue depending on your needs but the mixture described here leaves the finished piece soft and flexible.

• A layer of paste is first painted over the black plastic and the pieces pasted on ensuring they are all glued firmly to each other. Tissue papers, sheer fabrics and other assorted materials can be combined in this way.

• The glued papers and fabrics are left to dry naturally.

• When dry the compilation is lifted carefully off the plastic and it may then serve as a design or as the basis for a resolved piece of stitching.

• The papers may be drawn on first before being torn and reassembled thus creating an interesting combination of drawing and fabric construction.

The construction of the piece is an excellent way of enlivening an idea and interesting combinations emerge. Further drawings may be taken from these compilations and gradually the source becomes abstracted and distorted until a promising composition is reached.

Above: Differing qualities of white or cream paper can be effective when manipulated into a dimensional collage. Using one colour range helps focus on the texture and the cast shadows. (JL)

Left: The palm tree pattern seen opposite has been manipulated and enriched with hand stitch and supported on a dyed background fabric. (JL)

Right: This collage using a variety of dyed and textured papers is based on patterns on a banded tree bark. Several of the papers were spent transfer painting papers. (JL)

Textural & Dimensional Surfaces

The flat shiny surfaces of the platelets were achieved by bonding painted 'Tyvek' on to a sheer synthetic fabric allowing the heat of the iron to fuse, distort or erode . Baking parchment was placed on top of the fabric to protect the iron. These surfaces were applied to layers of felt for a dimensional effect. Plastic garden netting was fused and stitched alongside couched sisal and wool threads to achieve the additional texture. (JB)

Tree bark intrigues large numbers of people offering a range of effects from smooth, satin surfaces to craggy encrustations that seem to fascinate. Similarly visitors to textile exhibitions are tempted to touch fabrics and stitchery in order to fully experience the visual and tactile qualities.

Give yourself time to experiment with manipulating materials to capture the quality envisaged and to build up a dictionary of textural samples for future reference. Allow your diagrams and descriptive notes to help you. If a gently raised area is required soft padding may be appropriate where as high ridges may need additional wire or a heavily stitched support.

Fabrics can be gathered, ruched, puckered, rolled, pulled, twisted, folded, pleated, slashed etc. They can be stiffened by padding with cord, string, wire, interfacing, bonded layers and dense hand or machining stitchery.

Ridges can be created by:
• Making long fused beads
• Stitching fabric over string, wire, pipe cleaners
• Applying the material to 'Wireform' which can be manipulated to the desired effect
• Hand or machine wrapped cords
• Couched and knotted cords or thick yarns
• Line stitches - several layered one on top of the other. Romanian couching, raised chain band and chain worked in fairly bold threads can be successful
• 'Xpandaprint' (puff paint) applied to threads and cords can be expanded by applying heat and coloured with acrylic or fabric paints

Craggy, patchy effects can be achieved by:
• Layering fabric
• Layers of felt, heavy duty vilenes under bonded materials
• Padding using various types of wadding
• Fabric shapes made by machine stitching onto soluble material to make a new cloth.

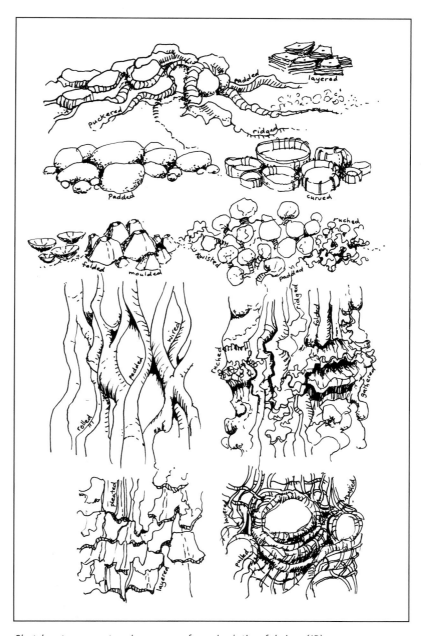

Sketches to suggest various ways of manipulating fabrics. (JB)

For surface decoration experiment with:
• Bonded fabrics
• Texture gels
• Fabric paints
• Synthetic fabrics including sheers etched or distorted with a soldering iron or hot tool
• Hand and machine stitching
• Painted 'Tyvek' or 'Xpandaprint' (puff paint) and other dimensional or coloured fabric glues now available. USE WITH DISCRETION.

Try not to use too many effects together as it may prove to be difficult to create a unified work with so many elements vying with each other. Remember to keep certain colours or textural elements running through to link the piece. Even with this in mind further action such as overlaying scrims, interlinking hand stitches, darning, applying dimensional paint or machining into and around some of the shapes may be necessary to blend and integrate all the elements successfully.

Along the right edge of the sketch, handwritten notes read:
greyish, white 'resin', ochre tinges dripping over crusty bits ... peaks/apart = ... like a pale custard over a crumble topping - icing sugar ... ays, silvery b...

Left: *The sketch of the pine tree in aquarelle crayons. (JB)*

Above: *Inspired by the sketch on page 3 this dimensional interpretation of the ridged tree bark was made by applying scrims over dyed pipe cleaners before stitching over and on top to develop the surface. Wrappings and knotted stitches were added to make an interesting refinement. (JB)*

Right: *An interpretation of a section of bark from a pine tree seen in Callaway Gardens USA. The tree had exuded a substance which had built up a crusty texture even more dimensional than the platelets. Layered and wrapped lines of raised chain band stitches were worked in heavy sisal and wool threads with wire, scraps of fabric and 'Xpandaprint' (puff paint) incorporated. (JB)*

Capturing the Mood

In winter, woods viewed from the distance appear more evocative and atmospheric with a gentle hint of texture, softer shapes and the range of subtle colourings is often surprising. Spinneys of young silver birch trees viewed from the motorway show unexpected colour. From a distance, silvery grey trees contrast with their tiny branches which are diffused and appear as a soft blush of dull pink and maroon.

In early spring a haze of ochre, dull yellows and old gold heralds the blooming of catkins whereas weeping willows sport the most amazing tawny orange tips to the branches, the colour often intensified by late winter sunshine just before a shower of rain.

The effect of snow, frost, new leaves, blossom on trees could all be captured in stitch. The following words may well suggest the subtle addition of colour or textural marks to convey the essence of the imagery envisaged; mantle, speckling, mist, haze, shadowy, powdering, blush etc. Printing and sponging fabric paints to colour the material, layering and cutting back sheer fabrics and adding some gentle stitching to integrate all the elements are some of the technical choices you can make. Always be aware of colour rhythms running through the piece and keep the tonal qualities from being too dark or light and upsetting the unity of the imagery.

Below left: *Aquarelle crayons, chalk and fibre tip pens were used to make the sketch of silver birch trees seen on a winter's afternoon whilst sitting in a traffic jam. (JB)*

Right: *Atmospheric interpretations of a winter hillside and blossom trees by a roadside. Masking fluid was sponged or painted onto paper to provide a resist before transfer paints were applied on top. When dry, the design was transferred by iron to a polyester cloth. Snippets of fabric and thread were bonded under a chiffon scarf (polyester nylon) to develop the surface further. Running, seeding and tiny cross stitches were added to highlight some areas. (JB)*

Velvet Trees - Distorting the Surface

At first the combination of velvet with a tree source might not seem the most promising starting point but the pile of the velvet can be distorted and manipulated in so many ways that it can work surprisingly well.

Synthetic velvets may be cut or scored with a soldering tool and the edges curl and distort into organic forms that describe the gnarled and crackled forms to be found on encrusted bark. People frequently carve their names on trees and leave enticing marks which could be incised into the velvet pile.

Synthetic velvets have a richness of pile which can be coloured with transfer paints in a beautiful range of colours which can be particularly effective for shiny and satin type tree bark textures. (see book 4)

Contoured layers may be built up with simple bonding and then etched into for textured markings.

Cotton and silk velvets may also be coloured and discharged for a variety of effects before being hand or machine stitched.

Silk viscose velvet is commonly used for devoré technique. Tree bark markings make excellent all over patterns for devoré velvet and the resulting fabric can be dyed in a range of subtle or bold colour ways.

A whole range of hand and machine stitching may then be worked into these dimensional surfaces.

Far left: The design for this sample was taken from a beautiful shiny tree bark at Kew Gardens. Pale synthetic velvets were transfer painted before being bonded into bands and machined to secure. Delicate marks were etched in with a fine soldering tool. (JL)

Left: A transfer painted synthetic velvet has been cut with a soldering tool before being applied and manipulated to a hand made dyed background. Machine stitching completed the piece. (JL)

below: Contoured layers of synthetic velvet were bonded onto a contrasting canvas which had been painted with acrylic paint. Machine stitching and etching with a soldering tool added the textured details. (JL)

Right: This devore velvet piece was based on patterns from a palm tree trunk. The silk viscose velvet was worked with 'Fibre Etch' paste and when the process was completed acid dyes were used to colour the velvet. (JL)

barnacles on an old piece of wood found on the beach

The Wood from the Tree!

There are times when the sheer exuberance of wood demands an extravagant interpretation. A piece of distressed painted wood washed up on the shore on a summer holiday was the source of a series of drawings and textured stitched pieces. The initial drawings gave the proportions and the information but textured collage was useful when exploring the dimensional potential. On holiday it may be necessary to be resourceful as there is a limit to the materials it is possible to take and often difficult to anticipate the source that will appeal.

Some tissue paper used for packing was ideal for describing the encrusted barnacle shapes left as traceries on the painted wood. (see left)

Sketchbooks are personal and everyone approaches them in different ways but the most important aspect is that the information should be sufficient to work on when the source is no longer there. Any notes or jottings that answer the questions which might come up later need to be thought about whilst you still have access to the source of inspiration. A large piece of encrusted driftwood washed up on the beach is impossible to fit into a suitcase.

The initial explorations with fabric and thread could take many forms, but a layered approach using a range of applied fabrics including dyed and patterned velvets formed the basis of these textural pieces. The whole surface was covered in painted 'Bondaweb' before chunky threads were applied and ironed on being careful to use baking parchment over the top to ensure a clean iron. Nylon chiffon was then ironed over the whole surface and zapped with a heat tool to expose the gaps and hollows of the texture. Finally, before stitching, some 'Xpandaprint' was 'bruised' over the layers and expanded with heat to enrich the incrustations. Hand and machine stitching in sympathetic colours embedded the textures into the prepared ground.

Right:- These companion pieces relate to the driftwood found on holiday. They are worked on a linen ground with transfer painted synthetic velvet bonded on. Caran d'ache crayons were used to create vigorous marks on the surface. The final textures were achieved by combining layers of painted 'Bondaweb' and fine nylon scarves with 'Xpandaprint' and puff paint. The encrusted look is achieved by building up the layers and expanding the puff paint with heat before covering with 'Bondaweb' and chiffon and 'zapping' with a heat tool to create a distressed and peeling look. Thick threads have also been bonded in during the building up process. Free machine stitching was used to integrate the surface textures. (JL)

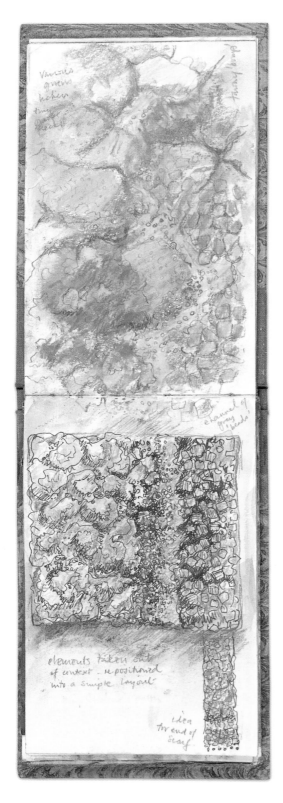

Three sketchbook pages showing a variety of tree bark patterns. Each one indicates, how certain characteristics have been selected and simplified into patterns which could be interpreted in appliqué, machine lace, patchwork and stitch. (JB)

These elements were arranged into a striped placement which could be worked as a panel, cushion or as an end of a machined lace scarf.

The diamond type shapes observed on a silver birch tree inspired the all over design suggested. (JB)

Stylising Patterns

Trees can offer an amazing assortment of features that could be adapted to form imaginative, attractive designs suitable for a range of items.

• Study some of your diagrams, sketches or photographs identifying certain aspects that really appeal.

• List in order of preference particular images or patterns that you like, accompanied by briefly written reasons. This action will help you select the main areas you wish to develop and may determine your first creative decision.

• Take elements out of context. Partner them with others taken from a different source. Arrange them in stripes, vary the scale, cut up and re-assemble. The design possibilities are infinite.

• Rearrange or contrive some images into the intended shape. Be aware of background shapes or spaces. They should be considered carefully too.

• Exaggerate or understate any elements. Simplify shapes and textures as appropriate.

• The actual colour scheme can feature although the patterns and textures could also be interpreted in a totally new colour way such as blacks, greys and gun metal or all in tones of gold or silver.

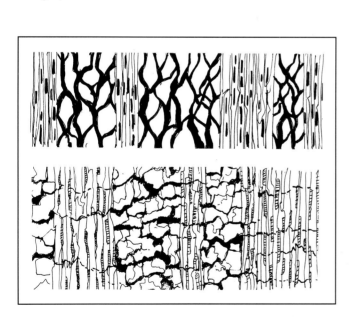

Stylised designs were created by selecting simplified patterns from two different trees. These could be used for borders, all over repeating units or cut up again and re-arranged haphazardly. (JB)

A prunis tree from China displayed an exciting banded tree trunk with shiny surfaces in rich reds, maroons and ochres. The simplified design was created using colour magazine papers. (JB)

Leaves to Inspire

Fruits, flowers, seeds and leaves offer a broad range of colour schemes which could inform a number of stitched pieces. For instance the impressive horse chestnut tree flowers are coloured in a variety of creams and soft pinks and might inspire a delicate piece whereas the vibrant red and orange berries adorning a Rowan tree would be more suitable for bolder work.

Summer foliage is a joy to behold. Notice just how many different greens that you can see. Apple, acid lime, soft grey, grey blue, bottle could all prefix green. It would be a useful exercise to match some of the colours by selecting threads, fabric or mixing fabric paints, to extend your visual vocabulary. Alternatively really observe a mature copper beach and marvel at the range of deep reds, crushed raspberry, maroons, rusty brown and purplish tinges. Looking up and through the leaves especially when the sun is shining brightens and lightens those colours.

Over the years, autumn leaves have been used to decorate shop windows, incorporated in collages in school or interpreted in appliqué, usually in a predictable way. It is accepted that leaves provide a wonderful resist when printing with fabric paints (see book 4) or can be arranged into exciting repeating motifs to create imaginative designs. However make a closer inspection of a chosen leaf.

Select a section out of context by using small paper frames. Identify the colours and their proportions. You will be thrilled with the unexpected combinations that emerge. Leaves do not stay in a pristine state for long so if there is not time to draw and paint them they can be colour photocopied. In order for you to concentrate on the colours, cut out the section that appeals so that the outer edges of the leaf do not inhibit your creative thinking.

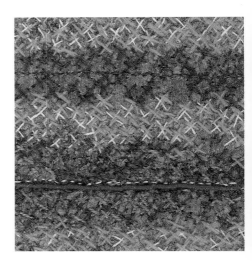

Inspired by these observations, silk paint could be applied to fabric in the chosen colours allowing them to merge with one another to obtain a subtle blend. Quilting or simple stitches could develop the surface further. Alternatively allow the colours to inspire some wonderful layered stitchery perhaps adorned with beads for a brooch, little bag or box top. Creating a cloth by machine stitching on soluble fabric may be another avenue to explore.

Autumn leaves were collected and photocopied before they became brittle and the colour faded. Sections were selected and the outside edges discarded so the colours provide the main inspiration.

Left: The stitch sample was worked in layers of cross stitch to blend the colours with back stitch and wrapped Romanian couching used to depict the red veining. This feature was taken from the leaf shown below and repeated to make a striped arrangement. (JB)

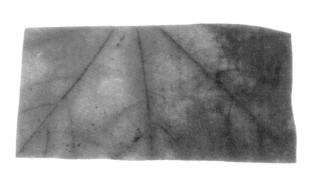

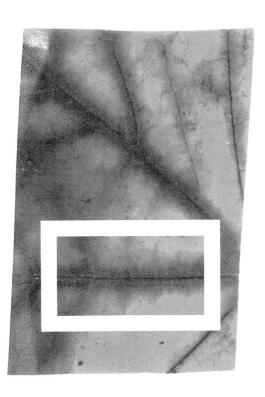

Structures & Networks

Magnolia leaves picked up in November. Fleshy leaf crust, delicate webs and films of decaying matter clinging to the skeletal shape.

very delicate transparent film left before decaying away

and the leaves turn into lacy skeletons.

A tree is a complex and amazing structure full of texture and colour and yet on closer examination an underlying pattern will become apparent and this will help form a framework for recording the observations.

As trees grow the outer bark crackles, expands and contracts into distinctive patterns according to the type of tree. Some trees have circular wart like growths in encrusted groupings and others have linear ridges that wrap the trunk in swathes of texture.

Contoured platelets contrast with deeply etched fissures and there are times when a quick sketch accompanied by words will provide the information necessary to develop ideas when away from the source. The veins on the leaves provide the backbone for the flesh that changes colour throughout the season then finally dies and falls in a riot of colour leaving the delicate veining as a fragile reminder.

Fleshy leaves such as magnolia and holly do not disintegrate as quickly as others and the decaying leaf material on the skeletal remains can be very inspirational. When the tree has been cut down the inner support system is revealed in the annual rings and these act as an archive into the history of the tree. These medullary rays also vary according to the tree but palm trees have the most fantastic and surprising patterns. Fossil remains of sensitive detailed leaves and tree textures provide another source of inspiration.

There are numerous ways of using trees as a design source but an emphasis on the structure could be an excellent starting point. Loosely knitted or knotted fibres can form effective frameworks for tree bark patterns as they have linked structures. There are various materials available that shrink or distort with heat and these can be useful when interpreting organic structures as they imitate the distortions of the growing process.

Above: A sketchbook page exploring the fragility of a skeletal leaf. (JL)

Right: Fibre from a prickly pear tree reveals an exciting network. This is part of the support system of the tree and some of the decaying material has dried out to form interesting organic patterns.

Far right: This piece is a celebration of tree networks. Two layers of knotted textures have been stabilised with PVA glue and fragments of fabric and hand stitching added to join the layers. (JL)

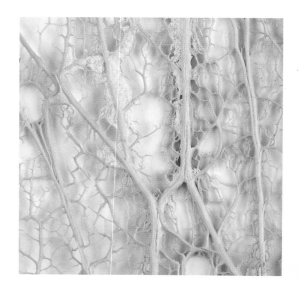

Conclusion

Trees as a theme is an immense subject only briefly touched on in this booklet. It is hoped that your interest has been aroused, observational skills heightened and that you are a little more aware of the amazing range of design possibilities suggested.

You may like to consider 'adopting' one tree to study for one year. Perhaps an old apple tree in your garden, a flowering cherry you pass when walking to the shops or a horse chestnut tree in your local park. The colours and patterns that change with the seasons, winter, summer, sunny or wet may well enchant, motivate and inspire you.

Collage based on a section of tree bark using magazine papers. (JB)

Stockists

• Art Van Go
The Studios, 1 Stevenage Road, Knebworth, Herts. SG3 6AN
Tel. 01438 814946
(Art materials, Stuart Gill, Jaquard, Deka Transfer Fabric Paints, papers, texture gels etc.)

• Fron Isaf
Angela Ramsey
Fron Isaf, Llanglydwen, Hebron, Whitland, Carms, Wales.
Tel. 01994 419523
(Hand dyed threads, scrims, nylon chiffon scarves.)

• Whaleys (Bradford) Ltd.
Harris Court, Great Horton, Bradford, West Yorkshire.
BD7 4EQ
Tel. 01274 567718
(Fabrics including scrims, velvets, Bondaweb.)

• Supermend - bonding powder
PO Box 300, Basildon, Essex.
SS14 3RT

• Oliver Twists
34, Holmlands Park, Chester Le Street, Co. Durham. DH3 3PJ
Tel. 0191 388 8233
(Hand dyed threads, yarns for hand and machine embroidery, scrims.)

• Strata
Oransay, Misbourne Avenue, Chalfont St Peter, Bucks. SL9 0PF
Tel. 01494 873850
(Fibre film - Tyvek, Xpandaprint - puff paint.)

• Husqvarna Studio
90, Lower Parliment Street, Nottingham. NG1 1EH
Tel. 0115 988 1550
(Vilene Solusheet - water soluble fabric.)

• Variegations
Rose Cottage, Harper Royd Lane, Norland, Halifax. HX6 3QQ
Tel.01422 832411
(Assorted materials, threads, Tyvek, Xpandaprint, spray web paint etc.)

Double Trouble Enterprises

Booklets in this series include:
1 - Vanishing Act
2 - Voluptuous Velvet
3 - Bonding & Beyond
4 - Transfer to Transform
5 - Gardens & More
6 - Conversations with Constance
7 - Trees as a Theme
8 - Giving Pleasure

For further information or to order please visit our website, www.doubletrouble-ent.com

Inside Back Cover: Painted 'Bondaweb' on a velvet ground with applied chiffon, ironed and burnt back with a heat tool. Enriched with machine into hand stitching. (JL)